Friendly Creatures

The First Friends of the Frogs Anthology

**Kings Estate Press, 1995
870 Kings Estate Road
St. Augustine, Florida
32086-5033**

— ACKNOWLEDGMENTS —

We thank the editors of the following periodical publications for their permission to reuse work first published by them:

Elf (Eclectic Literary Forum) for "Crab & Man," (Speer)

Journal of Poetry Therapy, for "Riding the Wish of a 'Horse'" (Cavalieri)

Pearl for "Nervous Guardians ...," and "Feline Leukemia" (Weber)

Poet Lore for "Bluebird of Happiness" (Cavalieri)

State Street Review, for "Of Yeast and Geckos" (Kempher)

Wormwood Review for "The Armadillo" (Kempher), and "The Animal Queendom," and "Cockatiel" (Locklin)

For work previously published in chapbooks or books, please see individual writers' listings in the Contributors' Notes at the back of the book.

Special thanks, as always, to Michael Hathaway, Jane Hathaway and Dorothy Pedersen/Wiley for their work in producing this book.

ISBN: 0-9637483-9-4

Copyright 1995 by Kings Estate Press
Ruth Moon Kempher, Editor

Friendly Creatures

Butterflies by Margo Hammond

from "Little Brother"

Butterflies don't hurt you.
No, I said.
Bees hurt you.
Only if you bother them, I said.
Wapses hurt you.
Yes.
Butterflies don't hurt you.
No.
I wish I were a butterfly.
Why, I asked.
So I wouldn't hurt anyone.

Carolyn Sobel

REQUIESCAT

I awoke this morning to the Lark Ascending,
Amidst the powerful pushing
of wing on air.
A single east ray
burning right eye orange,
its penetration forcing feathered fan higher
To the point of all beginning.

Linda A. Long-Gurell

TIDEWATER

Duckling boxes on the post office scale
As an ailing man mails his census form
Ours was on the motel room's doorknob
So we're registered for this decade's
Ratchet click it's been thirty-three
Since John Carter's church went up
Settlers here ten generations past
With slaves and indentured servants
Whose unmarked sandy graves are gone
We count with misplaced profundity
Should tally indiscernibles like luck
The rheumy man won't make next census
Anymore than this year's ducks.

D.E. Steward

BEE LINES

Bee stung me, broken string of Beethoven,
Bedazzled by her Botticelli smile
Bequeathes a friendly fire in her eyes
Because she needs to save me from her fears.
Beheld unbraided Beatrice, Dante's Blaze.
Besieged by words bestowed in martial time,
Begun Blake's Book of Thel, her golden lock.
Bereft of bride bethrothed to Pluto's beast
Behemouth belches key in swift retreat.
Beneath her honeycomb, a labyrinth,
Bejeweled iambic be-bop-lula.
Bewitched, the drone beseeched his beatnik Queen.
Beehive buzzed Beatles' "A Taste of Honey!"

Ignatius Graffeo

HAIKU

Ears ring with band sounds.
Each night when daylight departs.
Cicadas sing loud.

Claire Sorensen

MANTIS

Was it bird? Was it plane?
To the eyes of city child
nothing ever looked so strange.
Something brown, something wild
spread itself against the wall,
and the heads of passersby
turning, following its motion,
tilted upward toward the sky.

On that corner I had played
days on end, early bred
in city ways, in city tricks
but this was none of those. I stayed
still, frozen, as the brown thing
moved, flew down against the bricks,
displayed for me triangle head
great eyes and width of its spread wing.

I wanted it. It flew away.
Its image stayed behind
to prey on my imagination.
I never knew why mantis came
from green suburban lawns to grey
Manhattan — my house its way station —
leaving mantis shape and name
to take up lodging in my mind.

Carolyn Sobel

Carolyn Sobel

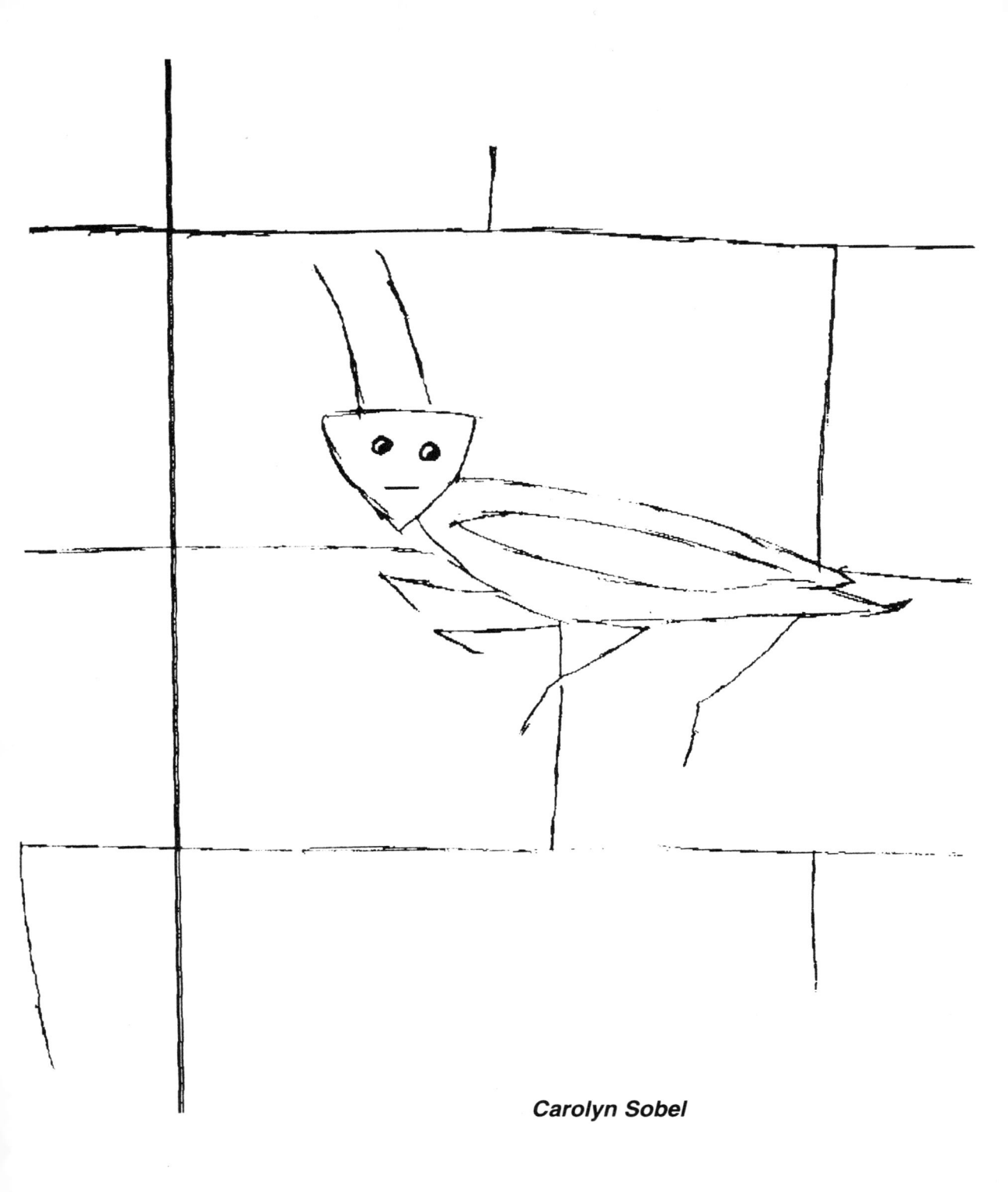

**CROSS SPECIES:
The Zen of a Young Cat**

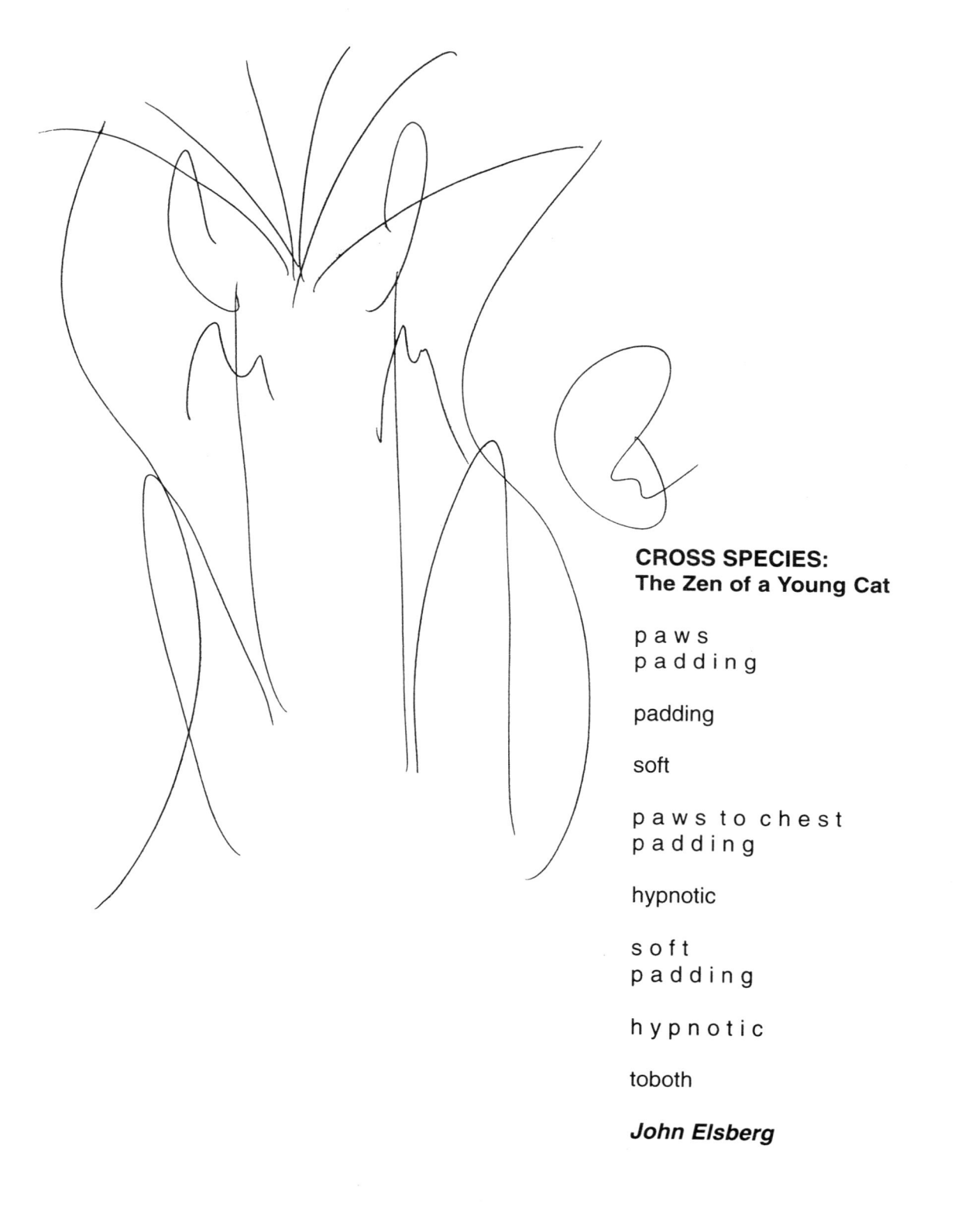

p a w s
p a d d i n g

padding

soft

p a w s t o c h e s t
p a d d i n g

hypnotic

s o f t
p a d d i n g

h y p n o t i c

toboth

John Elsberg

HOME BURIALS

Had Frost more than one suicide son, he
would have buried each one, with his rough hands
spread the dark soil evenly, craftsmanship

noticeable and necessary for
earth and sky to reach agreement. I have
no son, yet over the years have lost more

than one son. Lost father, brother, friend. And
today the small plastic bag I carry
to the edge of the planting bed holds more

than one heart. What is this? The tenth funeral?
The hundredth? When one lives on this earth for
some years, one loses everything slowly.

Slowly, each cat I saved from the lack of
human kindness lived its intended life
in what would universally be called

joy. Each shared the garden, and each remained
after death, buried at the foot of a
tree or beneath new shrubs. We bury all

things eventually. Our cities, our loves.
But the garden richly renews itself,
us, with this miracle of constancy.

Yvonne V. Sapia

JINGL

She always made me think of ancient,
  wondrous places.
She looked as though she'd been worshipped
  by a thousand royal faces.
And yet somehow when I brought her home,
  she loved me right away.
And she knew no matter where I went,
  she'd never run away.

I've never known such total trust
  as what she honored me with.
Yet she had such spirit that she
  could have been from an old Egyptian myth.

She hunted game of all kinds,
  rabbits, lizards, birds and mice,
and chased away any dog
  who dared to look at her twice.

Our souls touched for 19 years,
  love filled my heart for my Siamese girl,
and when the time came to say good-bye,
  mine was the last face she saw
  as sadness filled my world.

Life goes on, of course,
  I know it always will.
But I don't believe she's under the ground,
  not her, lying cold and still.

She's somewhere in a castle of gold
  with jewels round her neck, blue as her eyes,
waiting for me to join her there in a world
  where soulmates never have to say good-byes.

Jane Hathaway

THE BATTLE

Whiskers and bits of line twitching,
He waits, eyes my bait
And waits some more.

I see him there. Dark phantom
In the green-gray water.
I wait, pole in hand.
Today.

I wait some more.
Shoulders and arms begin to ache,
Muscles frozen,
Poised for action.
Hot!

I'm getting thirsty.
The shade that was has moved
Leaving me exposed
To the Kansas sun.
Maybe, not today.

I stabilize my pole.
Walk back for a drink of water.
Just as I raise the jug
I hear the snap.
Broke my line again!

I sense laughter
In his satisfied slap.
We both know, even when I land him,
I cut the line.

Dorothy Jenks

EXCERPTS FROM 'LITTLE LUCY: JUST A DOG (DOGGEREL FOR A MONGREL)'

Patrick calls her Toto.
Lisa calls her Benjii.
The Dartmouth Dog Officer
picked her up, a stray,
on Little Lucy Road, so ...
It doesn't really matter
anyway. She's stone deaf ...

She knows a kind of dog sign language.
Follows pointing fingers, comes to hands
that pretend to clap. We talk to her
and say it's telepathy. Walk her
leashed among mischievous pedigrees
and disobedient AKCs, cool
collected. Never a tug or tangle.

Neighbor children understand to not
sneak up behind Lucy. They have learned
responsibility, walking her.
One unhappy boy when he visits
relatives here, begs to take Lucy
out. They go to a place where they can
sit and there he tells her all his troubles.

Strange when I first saw you, I *knew* you.
Yes, I did. You are Albrecht Durer's dog.
His little dog in all those drawings, woodcuts.
There's Lucy curled at the feet of the
lady embroidering. Playing in the
"Chamber of Wonders" (where you're twins!) as the
collector shows it to his guests.

You are with countless hunting parties,
keep company with many of the saints.
But best of all: Running with your excited
face turned to us, under the body,
among the heavy tudding hooves of the
galloping, the huge, the white charger
on which your master in full armor rides —

to battle? Into artist's immortality.

Once curled pitifully shivering
on the pound's cold floor —
"No one will adopt *her*," they said.
Now she dogs our heels and
teaches us dogged devotion.
She is happy and tall and proud.
Small wonder, everyone loves Lucy.

Shivareee

SISTERS — AND BROTHERS

I cried for our good white face cow because I could not help her bleed or push throughout her too-long labor. I understood. It was just like when I had Jim.

"Don't worry," my husband said. "The calf's straight. They'll be fine."

The Mama tried to feed the newborn calf that could not, or would not suck. The Mama bawled out her frustration and I cried, too, as I tried to force electroplast, calf supplement, plain water, anything! — past the small locked tongue and clamped down throat. I knew what was needed. Debbie once almost died of dehydration.

"Don't worry," my husband said. "I'll give her a shot now and another tomorrow if she needs one."

The Mama bawled, but I calmed down. I remember the doctor poking life-saving IVs into Chelli's tiny pneumatic legs.

The Mama was right. We were wrong. The calf lay stiff and cold under the new morning sun.

"I guess we can't save them all," my husband said. "Help me load her in the pick-up."

I cried out loud, almost as hard as the bellowing Mama. But I understood. Suzanne was stillborn. Life goes on and tears don't bring the dead back to life. Understanding doesn't help much; tears come anyway.

The cow was a woman, too. She bawled — all the way across the home pasture, racing to keep up with the pick-up. "Fool durn cow!" my husband cursed, getting out to shoo her back across the cattle guard where she'd nearly broken an ankle.

"Don't yell at that cow!" I screamed. "This is her baby!"

Jaw clamped, he hooked up a hot wire to keep her out of the far pasture before jumping inside the pick-up cab again. Not once did he look back at the mourning mother. A half-mile along, he stopped, hefted the calf from the bed and placed her where predators would clean the fragile bones. Then quietly, he pulled out the last long grasses left from summer and gently covered the baby's face.

Margaret Shauers

* * *

DON'T UNDERSELL YOURSELF

Consider the brown cow
Eating green grass
Giving white milk

Grace Cavalieri

* * *

THE RESIDENT HAWK DOES ITS WIND DANCE

The redtail sails beyond
the world assessing
November 9th migrations
of warblers and robins
it stirs the sun and computes
moves like a stringless kite
it flies translucence with black fingertips
buteo stretched tight as canvas
in motionless deceptive trance
on stiff northeast wind
contemplating a kill
observe its rolling timelessness
fierce detached secret intent
hypnotically you begin
to think you are its slow revolutions
as if you both are caught in the wind
or corpses transformed to space.

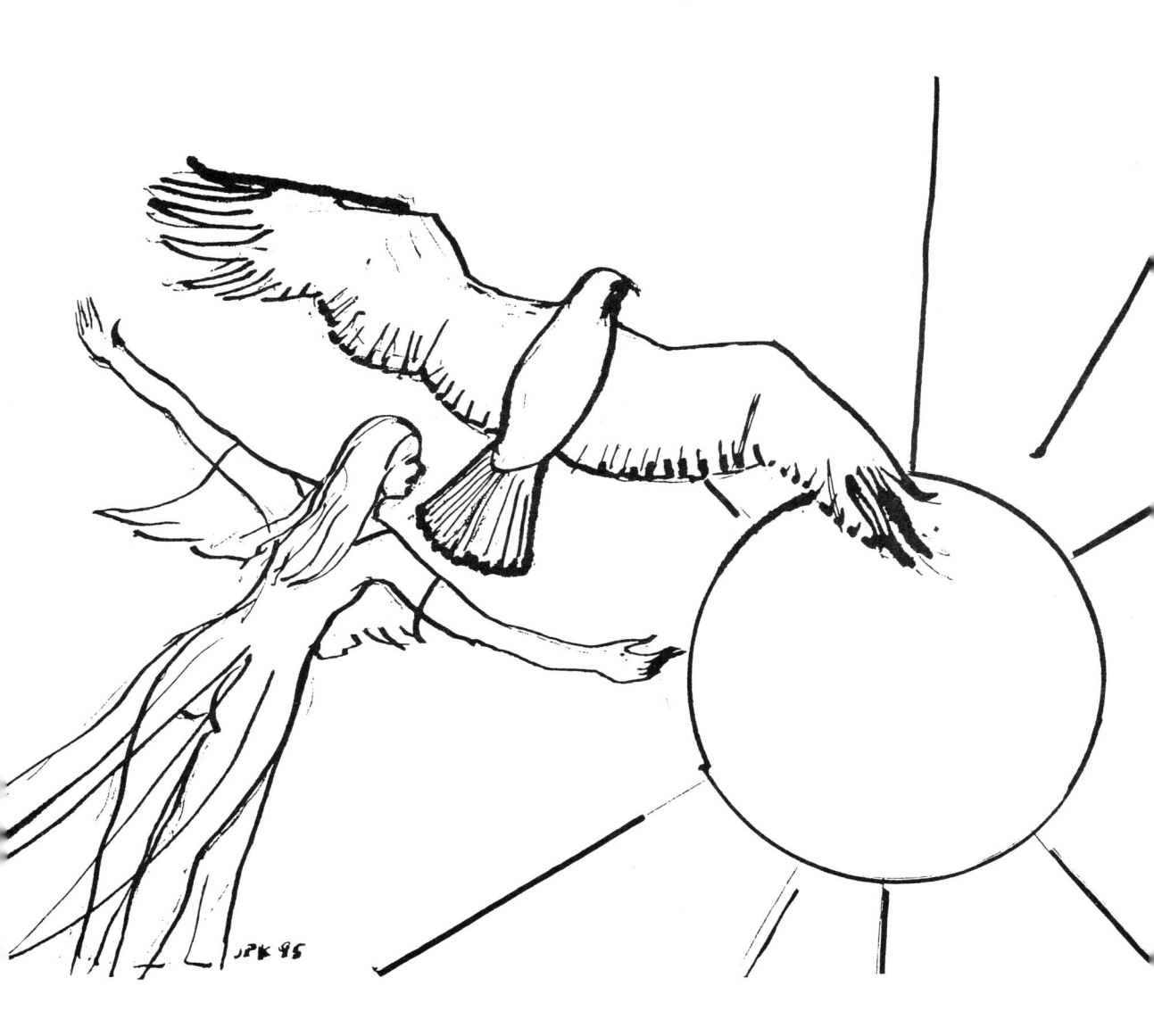

Joan Payne Kincaid

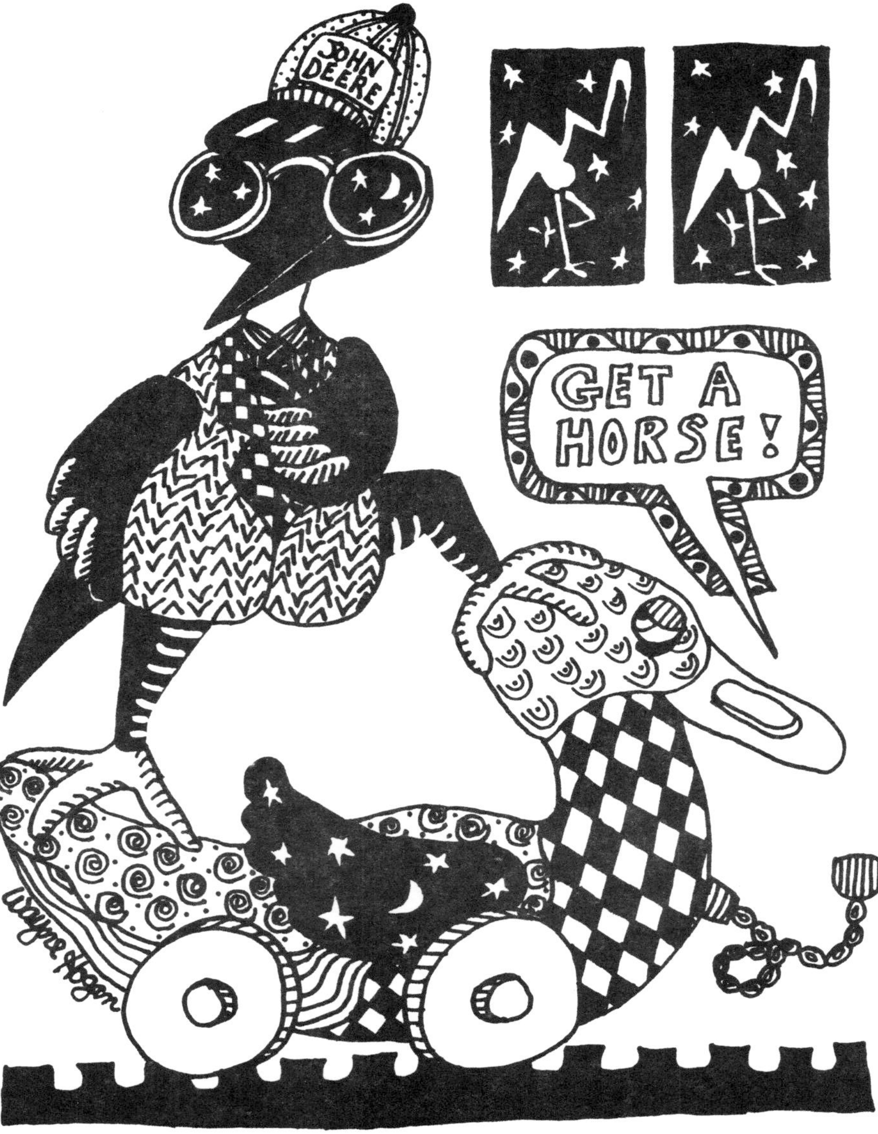
JOHN DEERE
GET A HORSE!
Wayne Hogan

PINK FLAMINGOS, ASPARAGUS TIPS?

Lamps give light
and horses, flight. Lamps
give light, stars, too.
Horses give flight. And pink
flamingos, asparagus tips?

DUCKS ARE NOT

Ducks are, no, not
necessarily placid. Ducks,
au contraire, can be quite, um
shall we say? agitated, can be,
well, downright arsonous at
times, can even gather their feathers
together and create quite a stir,
yessir, can, well, ducks are, no,
not necessarily placid.

PRESERVING OUR SPECIES

Clumsy cunnings,
minute duplicities hop
ecclesiastically along the
slats of rails. Above,
the circling swath
that's a crow, smiles.

Wayne Hogan

XANTHUS

Achilles got it straight
from the horse's mouth,
Xanthus told him to his face —
"You're a dead man, Achilles.
  The gods have sealed your doom.
  Patroclus lies slaughtered, naked,
  stripped of your iinvincible ploy.
  Stabbed by the sword of probability,
  victim of arrogant justice.
  The man never had a chance!
  Hear me out, O brave Achaean.
  Your trusted stallion speaks no Greek,
  But you understand the subtle glance.
  The gods play a game of chess;
  each man a pawn in their scheme.
  The outcome is always the same,
  vanity influences the best of us.
  It all for the glory of the gods."

Xanthus survived the seige of Troy
and later appeared in the 20th century
as the star of his hit TV series, Mr. Ed.

Ignatius Graffeo

-Ignatius Graffeo

CALLIOPE

    Flowers grow in great profusion on a meadow in a remote part of the forest. I go there from time to time and sit in the grass. I like to think about things.
    I live in a world of technological chaos. Men have walked the moon and I have a computer terminal which allows me to do my work at home. The children are grown, scattered and hardly ever ask for money. I'm still married to the same delightful lady and I've reached an age where there is less future than past, which I find more ironic than frightening.
    It was Friday afternoon when I headed out. In this part of the country there are four distinct seasons and, as the weeks pass, there are always new shapes and colors to please the eye. An unpaved country road wanders the valley. A covered bridge spans a stream, and there are deserted farms with apple orchards where I see deer and rabbit, but the part I like best is the woods. After the bridge, there is a fork in the road. To the left the road stays in the valley, but I turned right toward the hills. As the road climbed steadily higher, there were more and more trees. Maple, oak and walnut began to give way to pine.
    Under the trees it was cooler and the sounds were soft and secret. The ground was thickly carpeted with pine needles and no moccasin step could have been more silent as I headed deeper into the forest toward my meadow. Of course the clearing in the woods isn't really mine and I'm surely not the only one to ever find it, but I must admit to having a proprietory feeling about the place. I was almost there when I saw movement and bits and pieces of color through the trees. Who was trespassing in my meadow?
    I stepped out to confront the intruder and stopped short, my indignation forgotten. Sitting back on a long, slender tail, and tall as the trees, was a dragon.
    Now I know everyone has something to say about dragons. They're ugly, they smell, they're mean and green, or, worse yet, some say they don't even exist. But, at the far end of the meadow, where the flowers grew the thickest, sat a winged dragon, and it wasn't even green.
    This particular dragon was a tower of pale, shimmering rainbow hues that swam into each other. First one part was blue, then there would be a kaleidoscopic shift, and the color was lavender which became turquoise ... you get the idea. Also, dragons are supposed to have red

eyes and breathe fire and smoke, but this one had eyes of silver, like fireworks spangling a night sky and, instead of fire and smoke, his breath smelled of caramel popcorn balls. The dragon began to sing.

As he sang it was August and the circus had come to town. Over the noise of the crowd, the enchanting sounds of a steam organ reached the farthest corner of the field. The dragon's calliope voice filled the meadow. His song huffed and burbled and tumbled along, and the deep notes made vibrations on my skin, vibrations that tingled. I looked into the dragon's star-burst eyes and laughed. My knees were skinned, but I ran for joy and summer was forever.

Slowly the dragon and his song began to fade. Then he was gone and the day moved in again. A crow called from the top of a tall pine and from somewhere in the far distance came the rasp of a chain saw.

I sat in the grass among caramel scented flowrs and I thought about things.

James L. Diffin

FROM 'IMPROVISATIONS'

II.

Protected from any possible tragic event
we create our own jungle pride;
paradise for me is having 6 of you
following in a line up and down stairs.

We create our own jungle pride
trotting along from attic to cellar believing
following in a line up and down stairs
I, as the mother or some furless giant.

Trotting along from attic to cellar believing
maybe I'm the Alpha Female
I, as the mother of some furless giant
I, who attend to the food and discipline around this place.

Maybe I'm the Alpha Female
though I cannot execute wild leaps to the top;
I, who attend to the food and discipline around this place
so you can leap to the top of the fridge or armoire ...

Joan Payne Kincaid

SONNET IN APRIL

Invisible phantoms live in my cat
They change with the coloring of eyes,
Fortune has blessed, they're friendly at that
They hold the deceased awaiting new lives.
He harbors their souls in message divine
A calling by fate and grand design,
Appearing at doorstep I claimed him as mine
The chanting of angels in cat meow whine.
Plato in grey with four little white feet
Fur rises from ears like antlers grown wild
The movement of breath so gentle and sweet
I have taken him in to raise as my child.
With pleasure he sleeps curled behind knees
Ancestors cuddled in earthly release.

Gina Bergamino

RIDING THE WISH OF A HORSE

*If wishes were horses
all beggars would ride*

From the place of no nurture
I climb into a bed of birdsong
moving further and further away
from what matters

trying to write of not being strong
and to love the writing of it
with strength, with
resignation, like

a wild cat who needs the most
but can be touched the least.

In the distance, I hear it
moaning a constant prayer in the woods.

The house cats would have food rather than love.
They have surrendered early,
contented, like old women
waiting to attend the birth and death
of others.
The struggle is gone
what's left is just physical.

Grace Cavalieri

'FRIDAY' THE CAT

WHERE DOES THE TIME GO?
I LAY ABOUT AND WONDER
WHERE THE BOYS HAVE GONE?
MY MASTER & MY MISTRESS ARE HERE
AND TEND TO MY MANY NEEDS —
BUT THE HOUSE IS SO QUIET NOW!

THIRTEEN YEARS HAVE PASSED AND
MY BLACK LONG BUSHY HAIR
IS NOW TURNING GRAY — I DON'T
RUN OR JUMP OR PLAY LIKE BEFORE
I JUST LAY AROUND AND LISTEN
TO ALL THE BIRDS IN THE TREES.
WHERE DID THE TIME GO?

Dorothy Pedersen/Wiley

MY CAT THINKS SHE CAN BOSS ME AROUND

JP KINCAID

YOU, WE

You are
a mass of colour,
impossible
to disentangle.

You are
rolling down the lawn
fighting,
teeth sunk
in each other's throats.

You are
hunting together,
keeping level,
on either side
of the fir trees.

You are
told off
for bringing down
a blackbird,
biting the head
off a vole.

You are
licking one another,
tiger tabby,
pink, fine white,
rich, precious,
sleek, slick wet.

We watch,
we learn,
how to be killers,
Friends.

Patricia Duncker

EVERETT

Everett was drunk & sprawled on my couch at 2 a.m.
I didn't know Everett well enough
for him to be sprawled on my couch drunk at 2 a.m.
but my friend found him at the bar next door
waving a big knife around,
trying to fight with some cops,
so she led him away from a parole violation
to my house.

he couldn't stand up and collapsed on the couch
as he recited poetry he'd written years ago.

then he said, "you should be a dealer, man,
I could triple and quadruple your investment,
if you know what I mean (wink wink),
I'm going to Houston for a shipment —
your house is in the *perfect* location ..."
he pointed to his eyes and said,
"*Listen* to me, man ..."

My old gray cat Cecil jumped onto Everett's leg,
walked the length of his lanky body
and stood staring at him eyeball to eyeball.
Then he began licking Everett's earlobe.

Overcome with emotion, Everett whimpered,
"This cat likes me! I'm a lower life form
and this cat likes me!"

Michael Hathaway

"Pandora Louise Hathaway"

Z

Z is a blind cat
a decade old
he walks in circles
when he loses track
of where he is
walks around furniture
that is no longer there
it never occurrs to him
not to forgive the darkness
he lives bravely, fully
blue eyes wide/empty
climbing always to the
highest place in the house
with true Sagittarian zeal
he is generous to let me
think i am his
seeing-eye human

beast

(for Cecil)

pirate-eyed
July moon cat

funny clown
& star lover

wise secret
nightkeeper

tender chin
kisser

protective
nightwatcher

pillow hogger

perfect
life companion

NOT SINATRA

Cecil hates it
when i sing
he purrs for Sarah Vaughan
but not for me

his long gray ears
flip & flatten
on his rugged head
the tip of his
rodent tail twitches

his pirate-eyes say:
"I *have* killed my share
of squeaky little
animals ..."

**AS IF I DIDN'T HAVE ENOUGH
POETS CRAWLING OUT OF
THE WOODWORK**

i've taken to naming cats
after poets

so far there's shy and reclusive
Emily Dickinson,
tone deaf Stevie Nicks,
"Annie" Sexton, who has used up
more than her share of lives,

and the newest addition,
Sylvia, a kitten
who spends most of her time
trying to figure out a way
to get into the oven.

Michael Hathaway

my cat rose a

tortoise shell
w/a face she may
have stolen from
one of the furies
hates poetry if
i'm listening to
a poetry tape
she'll stick her
ears back & walk
from the room
what she likes
is chasing down
bugs i have seen
her fly 3 feet
off the grass to
bat a butterfly
beauty for her
is rubbing her
whiskers across
the edge of a big
bowie knife i've
shoved next to
my chair or
crushing a cock
roach in her
jaws she likes
to eat the juice

Todd Moore

MAMA DIDN'T ALLOW NO BLUES OR JAZZ ...

Lorne Cress

The monkey trap is simply this
A coconut hollowed out
A sweet potato stuck inside

This is how a monkey can be caught
He puts his paw inside
And grabs the food

This makes a fist

You say it's dumb
Determined as hunger
Caught inside a shell like that

You say betrayal comes from just
Such needs as a monkey has

We do not know the source of sanity
How monkeys feel about hunger

But I think it's better when holding on
From not letting go —
I think it's better to let go.

Grace Cavalieri

COCKATIEL

we'd only had the bird a week
when I saw a cat sneak in the door.
i leapt out of bed, flapping the comforter
and hissing, "shoo, cat!"

of course the bird went flying out the door.
my wife screamed, "fifty bucks!"
and took off after it.
she brought it down at the curb
with a flying tackle.

the cat was enjoying the show.

THE ANIMAL QUEENDOM

when the mother cat had kittens
i somehow thought she'd never leave their box.
i assumed that, except at feeding times,
she'd want to stand eternal maternal vigilance,
a monument to sociobiological singleness of purpose.

instead, right from the start, she liked
her little forays back into the other room,
even an occasional stepping out into the yard.
and now, just one week later,
although she dutifully feeds and washes them,
she much prefers to sleep stretched out
on the couch.

i figure any day now she'll be wanting
to go after her real estate license.

Gerald Locklin

albert york: reclining female nude with cat, 1978

(quadruple cinquain)

the cat
is large and gray
and blocky like a dog
or football player and its eyes
are flat,

black holes,
unlike the wo-
man who seems to enjoy
the attention, rose in short, black
hair and

one shoe
kicked askew, though
her breasts are small and her
torso's blocky too: the ghastly
cat does

not think
it is any
of our business, nor does
it have any interest in our
dumb art.

Gerald Locklin

PAPILLON SONNET

I'm a fourteen-line canine whose pedigree
traces back to the reign of Marie
Antoinette. In famous paintings, I'm the boa
of Brie-colored fur in her lap, the toy
spaniel protecting the Infante, essence du growl,
a lagniappe of a dog! Cheri, regard
these teeth — too small to scare a feather off a fowl.
I earn my keep by cuddling on a pillow
and cocking my head just so. No kennel
for me, non, non! Chez the Musee des Beaux
Arts the women who treasure beauty throw
kisses and the men bounce me balls.
I have no practical purpose at all
except to be a little plume of pleasure.

Enid Shomer

PLAYING ON THE JOURNEY

McDonalds biscuit egg & sausage
2 coffees for beach breakfast arguing in car
reverse decision to hitchhike home
manage the dobe and meal
crossing the inlet on a bridge-log
carefully side-stepping and basking
in island blue-green light
fog steals the view
of Connecticut
throwing a stick and an old shoe
for the indulgent doberman
humoring us
who we don't want
to admit is old too.

Joan Payne Kincaid

NERVOUS GUARDIANS OF THE DESERT CITY NIGHT

We have dogs all around us, who bark at falling leaves.— Catherine Lynn

it's a dogtown

yards full of them
yawping & howling
throughout the night
echoing their fears
off the moon

barking & protecting
the feeble possessions
of those that fill their bowls.

Fester, the one-eyed tom
weaves his way
down secret passages
gone for days
searching out
his fellow cats

in this dogland.

Mark Weber

jan 93

OUR CATS

Geminy though done with
her second dinner
is still stalking flies
catapulting into the air

Charlie i had to wake up
or else Geminy would have ate
all the microwaved chicken giblets

now they're both licking their lips
cleaning themselves rubbing
paws all over face
with contented eyes

soon they'll be asleep
and soon again, like the kittens
they are
will be chasing around
tearing holy hell
out of the place.

FELINE LEUKEMIA

the first frost
hit last night
and I spent the morning
working with the vegetables

a couple of weeks past
the autumnal equipnox
the garden is dying
its natural death

on my hands & knees
in one of the pathways
between the chiles, beans & lettuce
i pause at Fester's grave

and cry again.

Mark Weber

CANIS

Botswana desert jackals trotting by
Nuzzling each other like farm dogs
And frequently in the American West
Those New World jackal eyes but
To be just east of the Hudson
Coming up across a powerline cut
And spot an absolute coyote above
Staring me down in a reversion thrust
And then to scramble upslope to where
It had been to cast around for tracks
Or scat and then look up the cut
And have it peering down at me again
Was wondrously uncanny luck
Since to see dogs like that connects
To the stem of everything that all
Of us everywhere have ever been

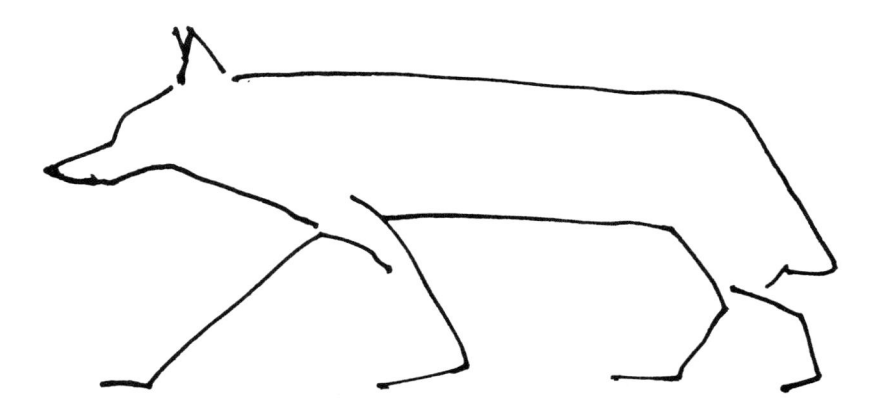

D.E. Steward

SALAMANO'S DOG

The first time you meet me, Meursault says: "*Il etait avec son chien.*" I don't care about the writer
or this sad, fragmented man and certainly not about
my so-called master. I only want to live beyond
this part of spaniel with mange. The old man walks
me twice a day. I pull, he pushes, beats me and curses.
So, of course, I run away at the first opportunity.

I slip my collar at the parade ground while he watches
a show. I know, it's Algiers. I might have a day
or night before an Arab slits my throat and boils
me for dinner. But for that one day and night,
I break the constraints of these dreary people.

I've broken out of this story.
Au revoir.
Adieu.
You wonder if a dog thinks,
plans, acts in his own behalf?

Laurel Speer

THE APPOINTMENT

Chu Lee gazed down at the floating corpse. He began to weep. The deep and bitter anguish tore at his soul. He had forsaken six centuries of unblemished tradition. Devout and subservient to the pride of his ancestors, he had failed. Lee fell to his knees and touched his head to the ground in final tribute. He lifted the pale, decomposing Koi carp from the pond. She had been a magnificent specimen; the only remaining productive female descendant from the great Ming Dynasty. The devastating parasitic infection had claimed its near final victim. The lone male was weak. It was doubtful he would survive. No matter. What good would he be without the brilliant female?

Three weeks earlier, Peking vandals had attacked his breeding pond and slaughtered the last of the queen Koi's offspring. Chu Lee found himself at the end of a legend. He had been chosen to mordantly inscribe the final words of its history. Silently and reverently, Lee wrapped the fish in the fine silk bindings that denoted royalty and laid her to rest.

Steam surrounded him as he bathed his lean, wrinkled flesh. The tea was especially sweet tonight. It would deliver him to the splendorous hereafter where his lord Ming waited in judgment. He felt no fear. Lee would wear his finest; the old wedding robe. It hung limply on his once proud and virile body. He smiled at a memory. In that instant, Lee saw himself as the lonely male Koi; floating.

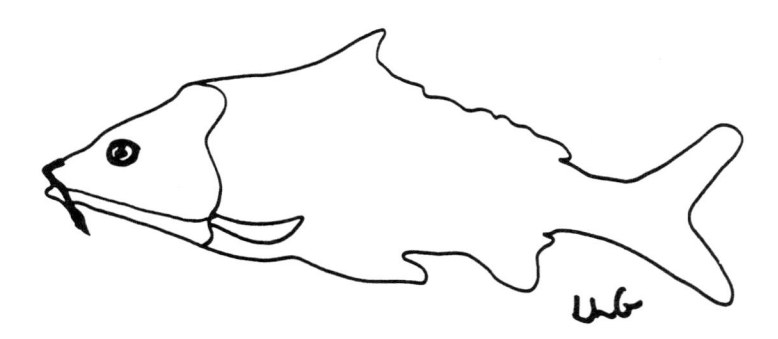

Linda A. Long-Gurell

LOGAN, UTAH, 1971

Nimble as the lumberjack
whose pocket-nest he deftly
left, the chipmunk scaled
plaid until he reached
the threadbare summit.
Then, with a chirrup,
he craned his tiny head
to survey the forest of
students who swayed
against the booming bass
of country rock, the wind-
chime of glassware.

Where the air is always musk-
heavy with spring, a little fur
goes a long way — and love
beads, letter/leather jackets
can't compete with a white-
striped tail that crooks
like a finger as the guitarist
gets down, calling co-eds sure
as shouts of "TIMBER" and the
curious silence of guilt that
always trails behind, like
an echo, mercifully muted.

James Plath

STALKING THE FLORIDA PANTHER

— Everglades National Park

Camped near fresh tracks, we wait.
Such blackness — the leafy horizon
closed shut like a fan.

The fire burns in whispers.
All night it has eaten itself
like a trapped animal

down to glowing red bones.
We lie on sesparate hummocks
in this river of grass,

the water moving
as stealthily as I imagine
the cat — its plush paws

dimpling the black muck
as it hunts. What I know:
that desire spreads like light

without doctrine. By morning
the sawgrass will shatter
the swamp to a million

glittering shards. Now,
moving for each other
in the darkness, our skin shines

like flares. I want to think
the cat is watching as our bodies
pull the wilderness in.

Enid Shomer

VESPERTILIO

for Sergei

In Mexico we honeymooned, my first
Time viewing the Pacific. Sunset dressed
A disenchanted evening as we dared
To peer across where barrenness can't be
As bearable as when, relieved by rocks,
Distinctive curving greens, one *sure* thing there
Reminds us our world hasn't been erased.

The moon stayed in. There's nothing light tonight.

Stiff bristled fear dug tracks in my scalp till
We plug extension cords in lamps, parade
Out on an Acapulco balcony
Like bridesmaids, hoping for some bats, their red
Machinery of appetite alive
This hour, ready to devour my edge
Of desolation. Batwings flap, a sound
Like crisp applause, but, spotting lights below,
Some hide a tiny face in their arms like
Shy children. It's so black, infernal all
Around, when this nocturnal choir rides.

Through wind, they speak to me, the antidote
To barrenness, forever pushing on
Despite the vast uncaring, steadying,
As if wings were springs that released my day.

LindaAnn Loschiavo

THE BLUEBIRD OF HAPPINESS

When they told us of the bluebird
          of happiness
with its rebirth, resurrection,
redemption,
we thought it was about the bluebird

because all along we were told
they'd only like us if we were
somebody else.

They forgot to say that death
is part of a perfection
where nothing exists
but what we take with us,

that we can steal conscious sight
from our unconscious soul,
a large hat with blue feathers
that fits no one else
and no one else can wear.

What trouble we'd be spared
knowing it can't be taken from us.
I'm talking about the comfort where
you don't wind up in someone else's hat.

With such knowledge as that
our surrender is like summer
floating in its boat.

We leave our sprinkle of blue
in the fields ...
But that doesn't mean
we will wait
until it means nothing to us before we can go.

Grace Cavalieri

THE BLACK-BELLIED PLOVER

Headwaiter: tuxedo,
black vest, white bib,
hauteur on bow legs —

He shows the single tourist
to his worst table
by the swinging door.

Between customers he slumps
into his shapeless slippers,
sags to rest against

the washroom wall, yet
always re-inflates himself
to scold the twittering peeps

as the dinner crowds arrive.
He samples the souvlaki,
tastes a sandflea here and there,

black eyes as personal
as Greek olives in a jar.
No one goes hungry.

The guidebooks say
a bird must eat
all his waking hours

just to stay alive.
When does he sleep?
High tide or low, it is

never between meals
at B.B. Plover's Seaside Cafe.

Chick Wallace

CRAB & MAN

Sometimes crabs will nibble the toes
of man or eat him entirely up.
Other times, man will put on the napkin
and chomp down master crab after boiling
him alive, cracking open his poor, spiny
joints to suck and pick the white meat out.
A nice wine, chilled, will enhance the feast.

When crab turns on man, there's no candles,
fine clothes, laughter and conversing
over dessert, but carbolic, commodes
and screaming for relief from pincers
eating the brain and heart.

Someone couuld construct a nice little fable
from all these happenings, but I'm not
in the mood.

Laurel Speer

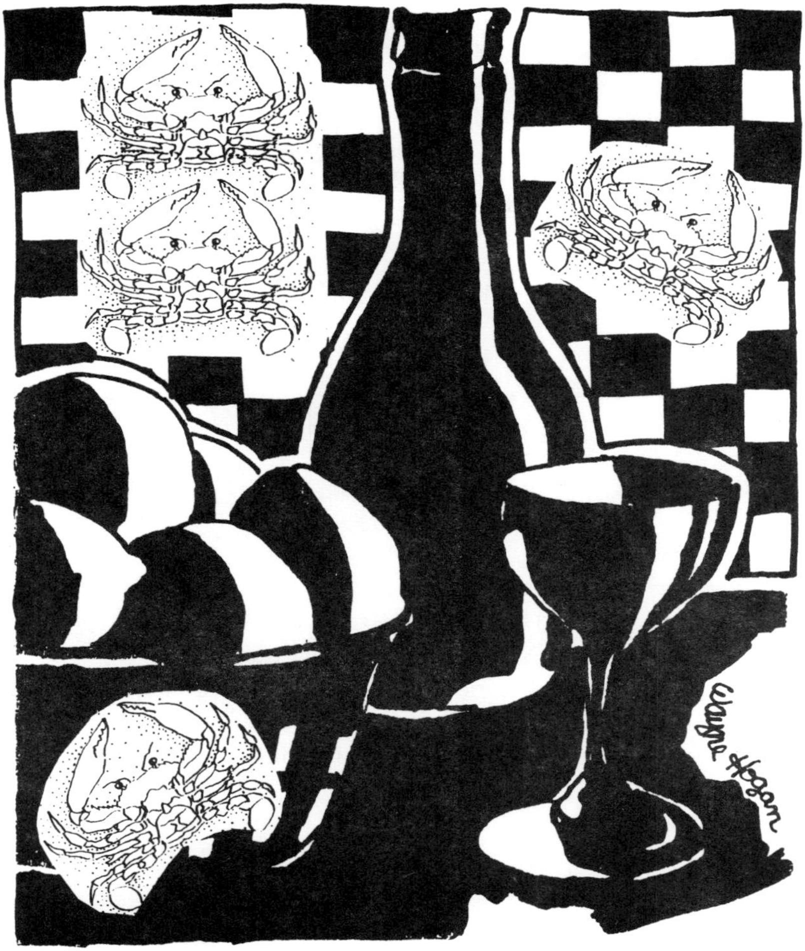
Wayne Hogan

THE PELICAN

She is:

> the gluttonous countess I saw last night
> on A & E in "Hotel du Lac"
> napkin spread under her chin, slavering,
> to gulp the goblet of port in one swig,
> to gullet down the whole poached trout in one bite

She is:

> the bleached-blonde fat lady
> in the chain shore cafeteria
> her peroxide bangs fine as baby fuzz, yet
> somehow new-looking, like a pelican's
> top knot, and then you know that
>
> what is growing out of her pink skull
> comes after the brain; tumor surgery and
> the radiation and chemotherapy
> and this is her first time out in public.
> She clamps her third chin low to mold
>
> the institutional green napkin pressed upon her ruined bosom.
> She has waited in line with her brown tray
> like a beak for her $2.85 meat loaf special.

Chick Wallace

A WHALER'S JOURNAL: WRECK

the boat shattered
was thrown up into the air
by the Right whale
the right one to catch
with baleen
& bone
& oil
lots of oil

I read this as dusk
settles
by the window
wind whipping
around shutters
I have left open
so I can look out
onto the bay
from this second story
see the sun set

the world of whalers
& fishers
& cowboys of dunes
is all before me
I follow the comings & goings
of ships
I follow the lights
the sunsets are of different hues
than my years West
in Colorado & New Mexico

there, there is a violet
a mauve
mountains thick & heavy
are suspended only
by sun setting or low clouds
the shapes blackened
& so distinct
there are golds
but rarely any reds

here from this window
I always see iced reds
but it could just be
how I feel
as the wind
picks up drops of the bay
& whistles around my shutters

I was reading
that old whaler's journal
about a boat shattered
& thrown up into the air
like a whirlwind of thousands
of leaves of oak
most of the men drowned
the whale came right up
under the boat
before the harpooner
& lancer
even raised their spear
as if she knew
as if others had tried

I was so close
I could reach out
& touch her
smooth grey skin
I looked for old wounds
in the perfect curve of her body
I found none
only the two of us survived
swam to shore
kicking our legs behind
shattered wood
built a fire to warm ourselves
& as I stared across
the sputtered flames
into his eyes
I asked very slowly
if he thought her beautiful
in her way
if he had ever felt such
a closeness to his prey
if he thought those
that had perished
had gone down
willingly with her
if he was glad
to have survived
to have a chance
to meet her again
one day

Kyle Laws

GULLS FOLLOW FISHING BOATS
LIKE CROWS THE CORN

I heard crows this morning outside the window
  & they sounded like gulls
  the shape of body
  of wind is the same
  the fullbreast
  wide wing
  strong head
crows follow corn in the fields
  even the winter stubble
  horses pick their way around
  thick manes & autumn fattened bellies
  along a barbed wire fenceline
on the way to the Deer Dance
  a dust white horse with thick throat
  rubbed its neck against a post &
  I laughed cause it looked like
  a mangy cat in spring
gulls follow fishing boats like crows the corn
  flags flying from the stern
  they chatter among broken shells of clams
  squawk & caw & face into the wind
  on thin poles dug into sandbars
I hear them out the window
  the day after Christmas
  cawing out about the rush of waves
  the white skin of birch
  entrails of whales
  littering the ancient beach
  the old hunting season
  snow on the dunes
  watchmen calling out from towers
  at the familiar spout from the blowhole

Life 7/95

    men set out from a winter-crusty shore
      in small boats that pound against
      the incoming waves like lifeguards
      red & white boats of rescue
      riding back down the tail of wave
      foam spraying hands & faces
      they follow the spout
      the blow
      the breath
      intent on the full round body of blubber
      & grey skin & bone & baleen
      irons raised
      as the rowers move in closer & closer
    as harpoon pierces skin
      the whale sounds for bottom
      pulling men with him to a shore lined
      with white streaked birch
    they will boil the stripped down skin
      in huge black pots
      lights from beach fires
      twinkling through pines
      gulls cawing out &
      crowding the entrail-strewn shore
      like crows calling from limbs of cottonwoods
      in the fall of snow from wind-blown leaves
      the winter stubble of corn in the fields.

Kyle Laws

VIRGINIA AND THE PARROT

The parrot had never been out of its cage,
The time that it happened the girl was enraged.
Tropical birds were uncommon back then;
Virginia was frantic as she told the men

"Wherever it's hiding it must be discovered!
It's there in the tree and it must be recovered!"
The ladder went up and the parrot went higher.
The scene must have piqued the poor workers' ire.

As one finally crept near, the parrot spoke out.
"I am sure a fine boy!" he said with a shout.
With youngsters all listening from near and afar.
Said the man as he grabbed him, "The hell if you are."

Charles Kelly

HAIKU

Flash of scarlet wings,
A shout of "Pretty, pretty!"
A Christmas card bird.

Claire Sorensen

INTO BED OF ROCKS

Under the palm tree
on the empty patio
in front of quiet pool

beneath a gray raincloud
she saw snake travelling low
sliding on its belly

into a bed of rocks
near hibiscus in row
as her own thoughts wandered

away from shifting breeze
to things she would not know
until she dived under

the motionless water
to start a wave or flow
greater than fear or doubt.

A FABLE

In semi-tropics
lizards on jacaranda
as two crow-crones change
building their nest towards the sun
impatient for flight.

The villa was named
St. Kitts, like their first island,
as they fluttered wings
recalling the memories
of distant passion.

Small-throat did not sing
while Flapping Tail kept dancing
from palm tree to palm
holding the warmth of coral
on Florida isle.

Rochelle Lynn Holt

FROM THE *LOS ANGELES TIMES*, PARAPHRASED

authorities said:
the endangered California condor
found dead in the wild
last October
was a victim of antifreeze poisoning
that the bird died of kidney failure
after drinking ethylene glycol
probably from a puddle
left by a leaking car.
the condor was one of two released
as part of the project to restore
the nearly extinct birds
to the wild.

another report tried to explain
that the Earth's population
will level off
simply if individuals DO NOT die (!)
that our over-production is
a subliminal response to
the Black Death plague.

have also hard that in 30 years
the human population of Earth
is going to double.

and i see where
Joshua Tree National Monument
is now swarming
with rock climbers —

humans, humans, humans,
everywhere.

Mark Weber

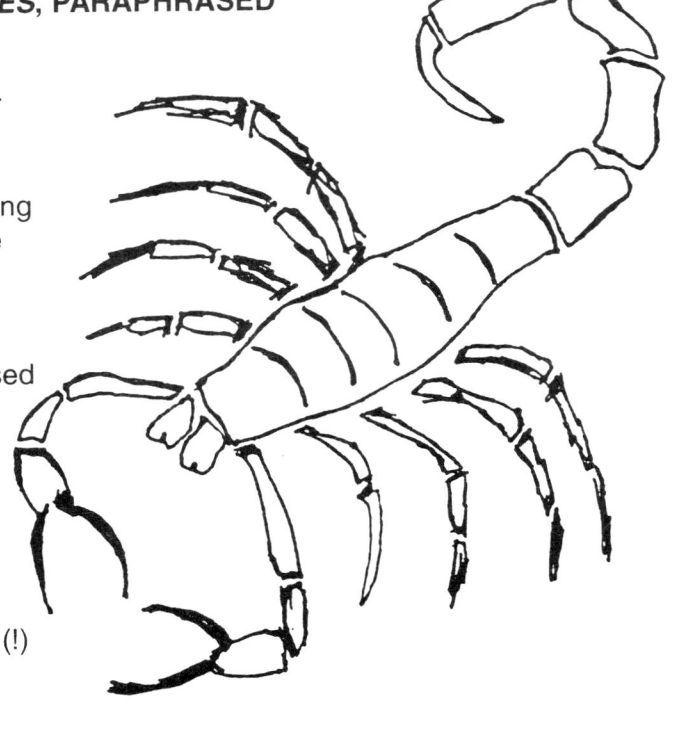

my friend Elmer

THE ARMADILLO

crossing U.S. 1, intent upon a faint but tantalizing
weedy scent, did not notice, but bearing down upon him
(from the north) a pickup truck with an electrician
well-equipped with ladders, wires and so forth, was
coming.
      Nor did he in his preoccupation note a
closer yet sedan approaching from the south: a car
which at that moment bore two aged sisters, who
had lately visited the Fountain of Youth, for
post cards and free orange juice —
                        which (car) swerved
and slewed across the median. He heard the crash. In fact
he curled his mouth at that, as two old ladies and one
not quite young electrician found themselves fairly
obliterated; their lives snuffed out, quite done —

the blame for which can be laid right squarely on
the armadillo crossing U.S. 1.

Ruth Moon Kempher

OF YEAST AND GECKOS

    It was
anathema, I felt, cursed
and lost — anything I touched —
the philodendron carried in, careful
against the frost, dropped leaves
heart-shaped, to sizzle
on the radiator.

The plant drooped, and then
out flew a young gecko
into my alien kitchen, groped
into dust-clogged mazes
under the counters, lost. Almost
        a whole week
lost, eating what?
tapping at cans and boxes —
hardly bigger, himself
        than the roaches, and I
no help whatever —
myself unkiltered, also lost.
A cake-mix solitude, left
to us both. Dry yeast.

        Driven by thirst
at last, the gecko flipped
into the dogs' water bowl
to drown.

        Its touch —
four sets of tiny fingers
against my arm — took faith
but he held on all the way
a blessing —

back to the porch, mild weather
    loops and hearts
of the also-returned
philodendron.

Ruth Moon Kempher

Joseph H. Kempher

OUR SHOCKINGLY DIRTY GARDEN

I want to come back to that garden with the toad
in it. For us, both of them are real.
The garden's gone wild, shocking disarray,
weed-choked, dry, chockablock with cactus and scrub.
We look out our dust-streaked window and think,
"What's the use? This is nature taking over
the effort to impose order."
The horned toad is perfectly hidden sitting in dirt.
We have to be looking exactly at him to catch
his placement on this scene.
He knows he's not toad at all, but lizard
with hornlike spines. Clver fellow to hide out
on earth in full view. His life is insects,
catching them for food, keeping his own kind
of order in the yard.

It's hot. Wind stirs the dirt, but the toad
stays put.

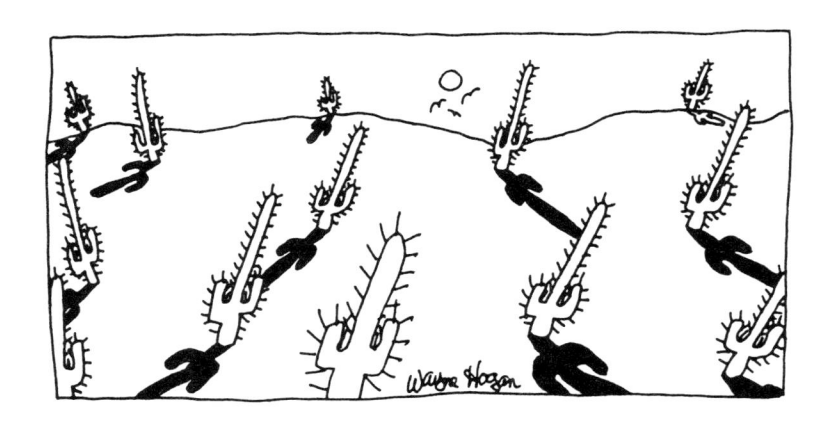

COYOTES

Coyotes ravage the hillsides, they say. The desert scrub,
crops, stock. These cocky, dog-eared packs can't be allowed
survivors sport. They laugh us to red-eyed rage and revving
of turbo-jet chopper blades. Sweeping low over daytime lairs,
we pock, pock, pock their lives away, mechanized hunters in
designer jeans running brown scramblers into the last cul de sac.

The end is a mountain of pelts still on skin built to a slagheap
of coyote death. The last male pup is stretched dried paws
to nose black for the eating eye of the camera, chopper set down
behind, a high whining horse monster. Not a game of croquet,
they say, and snort dust clots.

Laurel Speer

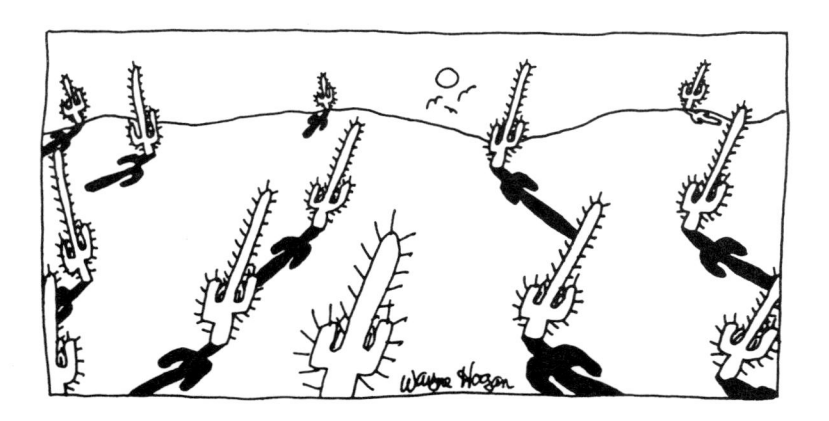

dancer of dark rivers

you know coyote he's
the one with the
silly grin sleeps all
day in the snake dance
lodge rocks all night
thinks he's got it all
figured out he's the
dealer of the cards
he's the butt of the
jokes he's the dancer
of dark rivers he's
the calm in the center
of the hurricane
drinking the stars
the diamonds of the
gutter always thinking
he's breaking free
but just once again
setting another trap
for himself

you can have my feet

take my hands, coyote,
here, take my hands
and give me your voice
take my earth and
give me your moon,
coyote, your
blood-circled void
take my drum, coyote,
with its goatskin
head and give me
your vision, i want
your vision, coyote
take my feet and
you can run faster,
coyote, they are
swift feet, and
give me your ears,
coyote, so that i
might hear the
whispers of those
laying the traps

Tony Moffeit

WARNINGS:
WHAT THE BIRDS SAY

Birds always know: Tiresias stirred
the guts of seagulls, told Antigone
she was as good as dead, who, hard head,

shrugged in ancient disbelief: "Old man,
you can tell nothing from the stirred insides
of birds. I'll go on doing what I want to do."

She did. Was punished, walled up in a cave,
wound up tearing her dress to shreds to make
herself a noose. She should've listened.

Today at Kesterson red-winged blackbirds
fall dead out of the trees at night in heaps
upon the poisoned earth. In labs young men

read the deformed guts of shorebirds, note
the absent eye, the missing leg, record
the shrinking migratories, measure

the dried-up wetlands, issue warnings:
"The sanderling population has shrunk
by eighty percent in fifteen years, faster

than any bird loss in this century.
We lose a dying species every single day."
The birds reflect our toxins and our greed.

While we who play Antigone, hard head,
unbelieving, ignore Tiresias,
absently shred our garments for a noose,

go on doing what we want to do.

Chick Wallace

EPILOGUE

Our staff has frequent seminars,
Don't think we don't.
We seek to present a product which is not only
Thrilling
But often educational.
Analysis is one way to discover what the audience may want.
Why just last month we had two actors dressed as frogs to teach
Our people mating,
But the female was to float on her back under water.
Now don't panic
We're not heartless,
She had a pouch of air just under her neck.
Don't jump to conclusions,
She was not tied down
Gagged
Or anything like that.
But it was the frog's nature
Not ours
And that's what scared us the most.
Would you want to do something against your will?
Well, how could you WANT to do something against your will!
Even though that frog had an air supply
The worry was always with us
How long would it last?
We dispensed with that project, leaving science to the scientists
And education to whomever cares.
We're not here to breathe under water,
There's not money enough for that.

Grace Cavalieri

— THE CONTRIBUTORS —

Gina Bergamino of Marrero, Louisiana, is a busy publisher of poetry chaps, with Big Easy Press; her own poetry appears in journals and books just about everywhere; she met her husband, Alfred — a fine pianist — while surfing the Internet.

Grace Cavalieri of Hedgesville, West Virginia, of the Bunny and Crocodile Press, does all sorts of interviews, reviews and radio work in the interest of poetry. "Momma Didn't Allow ..." was first printed in *Swan Research* (The Word Works); "Epilogue" was first printed in *Body Fluids*, and "Don't Undersell Yourself," was first in *Why I Cannot Take a Lover* (Washington Writers' Publishing House). Cindy Komitz helped with Grace's illustrations.

James Diffin of St. Augustine, Florida is a free-lance writer, specializing in novels; his expertise with computers has been most helpful.

Patricia Duncker of Aberystwyth, Wales, is a professor of English at the University of Wales, and also teaches at Oxford and in Paris, at the Sorbonne; she has recently had a novel accepted for publication. Hi ho, Patricia!

John Elsberg of Arlington, Virginia, has a charming wife named Connie, and a day job lurking in Washington, for the government; all this, and he edits *Bogg*, too. *O F F S E T S*, his collection of verse from Kings Estate Press in 1994, has gained wide recognition, and may soon be into second edition.

Ignatius Graffeo of Kew Gardens, New York is the guiding spirit of New Spirit Press, which publishes chapbooks and two poetry journals: *Poems that Thump in the Dark*, and *Second Glances*; he's especially good at designing chapbook covers.

Margo Hammond of Hammond Studios in Mount Pleasant, South Carolina, was cover artist and illustrator of Carolyn Sobel's recent book, and long ago, did the same for Ruth Moon Kempher's *Lust Songs and Travel Diary of Sylvia Savage*, from which the butterflies on page 1 are borrowed.

Jane Hathaway of St. John, Kansas, is assistant editor of *Chiron Review*, and the amazingly cool mother of Michael and Joseph. Her book, *My Angel and Other Poems* is available from Chiron Review Press.

Michael Hathaway of St. John, Kansas, is the editor of *Chiron Review*; he is typesetter without equal, whose work makes all our editions possible; his book *Ratboy, Etc.* was published by Kings Estate Press in 1994. "Everett" and "As if I Didn't Have Enough Poets" are borrowed from his book *stumbling into light* (Chiron Review Press, 1993).

Wayne Hogan of Cookeville, Tennesse, is an incredibly wonderful writer and illustrator who has a lovely wife, Susan; his first book of poetry, with his illustrations, *Five Quarter Moons Rose Over Egypt*, was published by Kings Estate Press in 1994.

Rochelle Lynn Holt of Fort Meyers, Florida, is the proprietor of Rose Shell Press; she has two chapbooks of verse available from Kings Estate Press, and many others, available from other presses.

Dorothy Jenks of Lakin, Kansas is married to a farmer, and has a beautiful family; her first collection of verse, *Patterns of the Quilted Plains*, is the latest edition from Kings Estate Press, and was a hit at the book selling tables of the 1995 Great Bend Poetry Rendezvous.

Charles Kelly of Grosse Pointe, Michigan, who has studied at Oxford, is a strategic planner; his parrot poem is based on a family fable from the 1920's.

Joseph H. Kempher who was born — like our hero, James Dean — in Fairmount, Indiana, left his pen-and-ink drawing of a gecko with his ex-wife.

Ruth Moon Kempher of St. Augustine, Florida, had a great deal of fun putting together this collection.

Joan Payne Kincaid of Sea Cliff, New York, is a poet and illustrator whose work has been widely published; she will have a book for Kings Estate Press in the spring of 1996.

Kyle Laws of Pueblo, Colorado, has been writing a lot lately, about the east coastal New Jersey of her youth; summer of 1996 has a book from her and Tony Moffeit penciled in.

Gerald Locklin of Long Beach, California, teaches, writes, dances a little, reads a lot, and lately has been doing many poems based on his observations of paintings; his *Big Man on Canvas*, from Slipstream in Niagara Falls, New York, is particularly fine.

Linda Long-Gurell of St. Augustine, Florida, is a deceptively lovely lady who writes fantastic, lascivious novels about leviathans. We couldn't find room, but if we could ...

LindaAnn Loschiavo, a native New Yorker, is a widely published poet-writer, who writes reviews for New Spirit Press and others; "Vespertilio" is based on memories of her long ago honeymoon on the Pacific coast of Mexico.

Tony Moffeit of Pueblo, Colorado frequently performs his poems with drum accompaniment, which drives ladies and young children wild; it's whispered that if you don't behave while he chants his New Orleans poems, he'll have Chicken Man come git you. That may be true.

Dorothy Pedersen/Wiley of St. Augustine, Florida, does all the dirty work at Kings Estate Press; she has five sons, and the grandchild count keeps growing; her book of poems, *Yellow Bricks*, was published by Brent, of Wichita, Kansas.

James Plath of Bloomington, Illinois, is editor of *Clockwatch Review*, and is a basesball fan with special knowledge of Babe Ruth; he's also active with the Hemingway doings, down in Key West, and is a recent groom, so he's forgiven for not having time to draw chipmunks.

Yvonne Sapia of Lake City, Florida, is a professor of English at Lake City Community College, and is the author of a novel, *Valentino's Hair*, and of several excellent books of poetry.

Joe Sarnowski of St. Augustine, Florida, is a student who works in the Library of St. Johns River Community College; his dragon and chipmunk are appreciated.

Margaret Shauers of Great Bend, Kansas, is a board member of the Great Plains Writers Association, and has been known to buy drinks and hamburgers at the Holiday Inn bar, for poor, hungry poets.

Shivaree is the *nom de plume* of a dear friend, who would rather enjoy life in Sandwich, Massachusetts, without being fussed at by people who write contributors' notes.

Enid Shomer of Gainesville, Florida, is the author of several fine books; "Stalking the Florida Panther" is the title poem from her prize-winning work, published by Word Works.

Carolyn Sobel of Rockville Centre, New York, is a professor of Linguistics at Hofstra University; her book *Intermissions* was recently published by Kings Estate Press; she has lovely cats but the cats were taking over this book ...

Claire Sorensen of Great Bend, Kansas, is a board member of Great Plains Writers Association; she has a fine book of her verses, which she illustrated herself — many of them show a child's lively perception and wit.

Laurel Speer of Tucson, Arizona, is a contributing editor of *Small Press Review* for which she writes perspicacious reviews and articles; her poem "Coyotes" was first published in *T. Roosevelt Tracks the Last Buffalo* (Rhiannon Press, 1982) and "Crab & Man" is from *The*

Destruction of Lions (Geryon Press).

D.E. Steward of Princeton, New Jersey, also remembers old times in Trenton; he's widely published, and like many of us, is often found in *Abbey*, whose 25th anniversary we salute.

Chick Wallace of Gainesville and Crescent Beach, Florida, no longer teaches college, but is busier than ever with various projects, especially those involving conservation; her bird poems used here are taken from a much larger, fine collection.

Mark Weber of Albuquerque, New Mexico, has a new Fester poem, which he read at the 1995 Great Bend Poetry Rendezvous, and which will be to blame if there is a *Son of Friendly Creatures*, next year.